Long Ago and Far Away

Contents

Glossary

compass
A compass is used to let people know which direction they are facing – north, east, south, or west.

Egypt
Egypt is a country. Egypt is in Africa.

India
India is a country. India is in Asia.

London
London is the capital city of England. England is in Europe.

Pacific Islands
The Pacific Islands is the name given to all the islands in the Pacific Ocean.

Persia
Persia was the country now known as Iran. Iran is a country in the Middle East.

Peru
Peru is a country in South America.

**Before you read
the book, do you know what
these words mean?**

pharaoh
A name given to the kings in Egypt, long ago.

raft
A raft is made out of wood and floats on water.

ration books
People in England were given ration books during
World War II. This was because there wasn't much
food to buy. People could not go out to buy any food
they wanted. People had to share out the food. Ration
books showed how much food people could have.

tomb
A tomb is where the Egyptians put the mummies of
their dead kings long ago.

wireless
A wireless is the old name for a radio.

World War II
World War II started in 1939. Many countries in
the world took part in this war. World War II ended
in 1945.

Tutankhamen's

Tomb

Written by
Elizabeth Hookings

Tutankhamen (Tu tan kom un)
was the king of Egypt
many, many years ago.
The kings of Egypt
were called pharaohs (fair ohs).
Tutankhamen was just a boy
when he became a pharaoh.
He was about nine years old.

Tutankhamen died
when he was about 18 years old.
People don't know why he died.

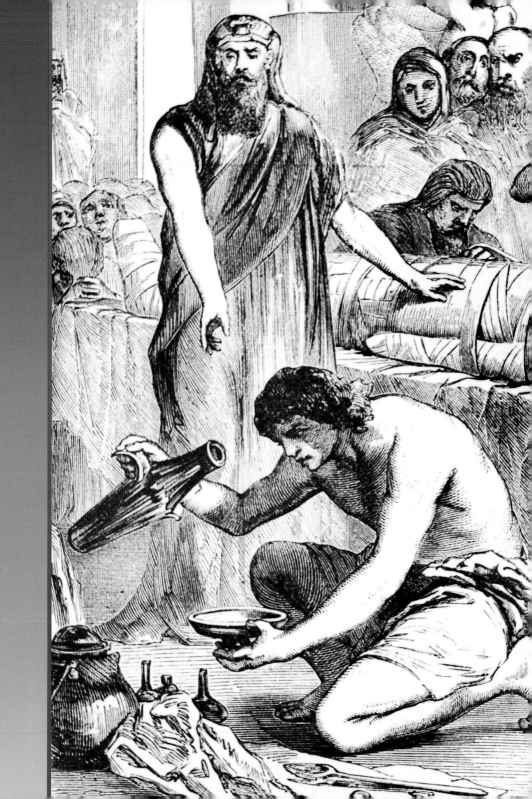

The Egyptians used to try
to make the bodies
of dead people last.
They dried out the bodies
and wrapped them up.
These bodies
are called mummies.
Tutankhamen's mummy
was found 3,000 years
after he died!
The king's face
had a gold mask on it.
The mummy was in
a box made of gold.

It took around 70 days
to make a mummy.
The Egyptians took out
all the inside of the body.
They left in the heart
and the kidneys.
They put a hook
up the nose
to pull the brain out.
They filled the body
with sawdust.
They dried the body
and wrapped it.
Then they put it into a box.

Could you
tell a friend
how to make
a mummy?

The Egyptians built tombs
for the mummies of their kings.
They put the kings' jewels
and many things,
like their thrones, in the tombs.
They put their bodies into the tombs.
The Egyptians used to think
there was an afterlife
that people went to
after they died.
They used to put all the things
the kings would need
for the afterlife into their tombs.

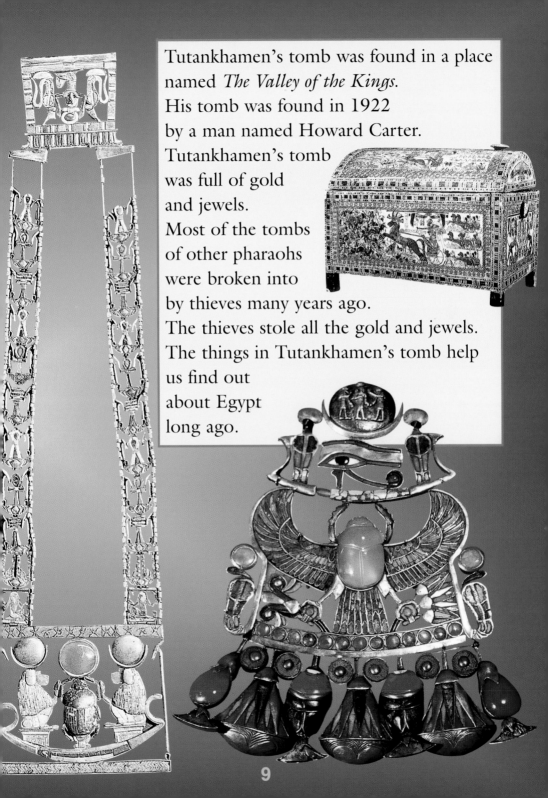

Tutankhamen's tomb was found in a place named *The Valley of the Kings*.
His tomb was found in 1922 by a man named Howard Carter.
Tutankhamen's tomb was full of gold and jewels.
Most of the tombs of other pharaohs were broken into by thieves many years ago.
The thieves stole all the gold and jewels.
The things in Tutankhamen's tomb help us find out about Egypt long ago.

Thor Heyerdahl's Dream

Written by Tracey Reeder
Illustrated by Nina Price

Thor Heyerdahl
liked to find out about things.
He wanted to find out
how the Polynesian people
got to the Pacific Islands.
He thought that the Polynesian people
must have come from Peru,
in South America, on rafts.

ASIA

NORTH AMERICA

Pacific Ocean

SOUTH AMERICA
Peru

AUSTRALIA

Pacific Islands

Thor Heyerdahl wanted
to show people he was right.
He said he would sail to the islands
the way that the Polynesian people did
a long, long time ago.
Many people said it could not be done,
but some men said they would help him.

Making the Raft

First, the men had to build a raft.
The men used big tree trunks for the raft.
They used nine trunks.
They tied them together with vines.

The men used little tree trunks.
They used little trunks to make a hut.
They put the hut on the raft.
Then they made two masts and a sail.
The sail would make the raft
move faster in the water.

Setting Sail

What could you use to build a raft today?

Thor Heyerdahl and his crew
called the raft the *Kon-Tiki*.
They got together lots of things
they would need on the raft.
They took food and water.
They took a compass and a radio
so that they could tell people
where they were.
They also took books
so they could write about their trip.
Soon, it was time to go.
Many people came to say good-bye.
Many people did not think
that they would see the men again.

At Sea

Can you make a list of the things the men did each day?

The days on the raft went by fast.
Each day, the men made sure
the raft was still strong.
One day, they saw a big shark in the sea.
It was near the raft.
The men killed the shark for food.
It took a long time
to get the shark up on the raft.
The men ate the shark.

Land!

One day when Thor Heyerdahl
was looking out to sea,
he saw some birds.
He said the birds would be near land.
So the men knew they were near land, too.
Soon, they saw the land,
but there were big waves
and they could not get the raft to the shore.
The men were very sad because
they could not get to the beach.

The men sailed away again.
A long time later,
the men saw some more land.
This time, some people from the land
came out to the *Kon-Tiki* in their own boats.

Shipwreck!

Thor Heyerdahl and his crew
didn't stay with these people.
They set out to sea again.
Soon, the waves were getting bigger and bigger.
The men could see more land,
but there were lots of big rocks in the water.
The waves were so big,
the *Kon-Tiki* went up onto the rocks
and broke.

The raft was broken, but the men were safe.
Thor and his crew took their things from the raft.
They put them onto the sand.
They looked for people,
but there was no one on the island.

> **What have you learned about the Kon-Tiki voyage?**

Journey's End

Thor Heyerdahl used his radio
to tell people where they were.
A boat came to get them.
It took them to another island.
Lots of people lived on this island.
These people were Polynesian people.

Soon a big boat came
to take Thor Heyerdahl and his crew home.
The men had made it from Peru to the Pacific Islands.
They were all very happy.
"I knew we could do it!" Thor Heyerdahl said.

SOUTH AMERICA

Peru

sea currents

sea currents

Tahiti

Pacific Islands

Pacific Ocean

Alexander the Great

Written by Tom Pipher
and Bob Eschenbach
Illustrated by Kelvin Hawley

Alexander the Prince

Many, many years ago
there was a small boy named Alexander.

Alexander liked to run and play,
but he also liked to read.
He liked to read books.
He read lots and lots of books.
He read books about lots of things.
Most of all, Alexander liked to read books
about people who lived in lands far away.

Alexander had a very good teacher.
His teacher was called Aristotle (Ar i stot el).
Aristotle showed Alexander
how to think and how to learn.

Alexander liked to learn.
He learned lots and lots of things
that he would do when he was the king.

Alexander also liked to dream.
His dream was to take over the world.

What things would Alexander need to learn?

Alexander the Smart One

One day, a man with a horse
came to the king.
This horse was a wild horse.
Some of the king's soldiers
tried to ride the horse.
But the horse kicked and kicked,
and the men fell off.
Alexander bet his father
that he could ride the horse.
His father said that if he could
ride the horse, he could keep it.

All the king's soldiers
laughed and laughed.
But Alexander was smart.

Alexander knew how to think.
He could see that the horse
didn't like its own shadow.
So Alexander turned the horse around
so that it faced the sun.
This way it could not see its own shadow.
Then Alexander got up on the horse's back.
He rode the horse into the sun
so that it wasn't scared.
Alexander got to keep the horse.

Can you find out what Alexander called his horse?

Alexander the Man

When Alexander grew up,
he set about making
his dream of taking over
the world come true.
He found out from the soldiers
how to plan and win wars.

Alexander found out how
to become the King of Persia.
He saw that the King of Persia
did not lead his soldiers into the war.
The king was scared.
He stayed at the back.
Alexander found a way
through the soldiers, to the king.
The king was scared of Alexander
and ran away.

Alexander found out, too,
how to become the King of Egypt.
He did not go to war with Egypt.
He built the Egyptians a big city
called Alexandria.
The Egyptians
liked the big city of Alexandria,
so they made Alexander their king.

Alexander found out how
to become the King of India.
The Indian army was a big army.
It had lots of soldiers
and more than 200 war elephants.
Alexander's soldiers had horses,
so they were much faster.
They won the war.

Alexander was not always fighting.
He did lots of good things, too.
He built cities and roads.
He built libraries.
He showed people how to live
when they were not fighting.

Alexander died when he was only 33 years old.
He was a very smart man.
He had shown the world
that he could win wars.
But he had also shown the world
how to live together
and learn from each other.

He once said,
"It is a lovely thing to live with courage
  and to die leaving an everlasting fame."

Devon
England
July 1941

Letters Home

Jacqueline Crompton Ottaway
Illustrated by Linette Porter

Dear Mummy,

This is a letter to let you know that I got to Devon.
I think I am going to be all right here.
I have a little room upstairs,
right up in the roof.

Mr and Mrs Black are very nice to me.
They told me they will look after me until the war is over.
It is nice they said that,
but I want to be at home with you and Daddy.
I want the war to be over.

Mr and Mrs Black have a wireless.
It tells us all about the night bombings over London.
I am sad you are in the big city.
I am sad you have to walk to work
down the bombed streets.
Do you pull the blackout curtains
over the windows at night?
Please be careful, Mummy.

Write to me soon.

Lots of love,
Sophie

PS Brown Bear sends his love.

Devon
England
August 1941

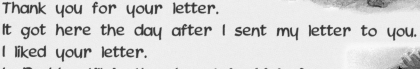

Dear Mummy,

Thank you for your letter.
It got here the day after I sent my letter to you.
I liked your letter.
Is Daddy still in the desert in Africa?
Are those bombs still falling on London?

In my bedroom, I shut my eyes
and think that you and Daddy are both coming to see me.
I show you the house and my bedroom.
I show you the vegetables I have grown
and the pond in the garden.

If you came to see me,
I could take you to my new school.
We are putting on a play.
It's fun to be in a play.
I like being in the play best of all.

Do you think I can come
to live in London again soon?
I want to be with you and Daddy.
Please write soon.
I do miss you a lot.

Lots of love,
Sophie

Devon
England
September 1941

Dear Mummy,

I got your letter today.
I read it over and over again.
It was a nice letter.
I know you and Daddy love me.
I know that is why I am in Devon until after the war.

I also got a letter from Auntie Margaret today.
It is a long letter.
She said, "Your mum was the best worker
at the factory.
She and a few other people had to stay late last night.
Your mum was going home when the bomb fell."

Mummy, I'm so sad.
I have been crying a lot.
Please write soon.
Please tell me you are all right.
I love you, Mummy.

Lots of love,
Sophie and Brown Bear

Facts about World War II in England

Did you know?
Lots of parts of London were bombed.

Did you know?
In the war there were blackouts.
In blackouts, people had to turn off all the lights and put black curtains over their windows.
This was to stop the bomber pilots from seeing the towns.

27

28

Did you know?
Many women went out to work.
They worked on the land
and in factories.

Did you know?
Many people built bomb shelters under the ground at home.

Did you know?
Lots of things were rationed. Everybody was given ration books. The ration books said what people could buy. Many people grew their own food, too.

Some people kept chickens and cows to give them eggs

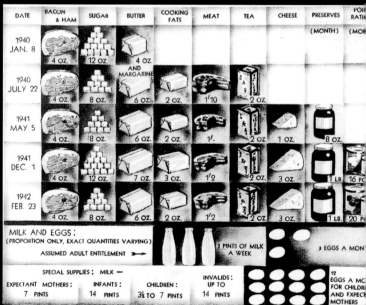

DATE	BACON & HAM	SUGAR	BUTTER	COOKING FATS	MEAT	TEA	CHEESE	PRESERVES (MONTH)	POII RATI (MON
1940 JAN. 8	4 OZ.	12 OZ.	4 OZ. AND MARGARINE						
1940 JULY 22	4 OZ.	8 OZ.	6 OZ.	2 OZ.	1'10	2 OZ.			
1941 MAY 5	4 OZ.	8 OZ.	6 OZ.	2 OZ.	1'.	2 OZ.	1 OZ.	8 OZ.	
1941 DEC. 1	4 OZ.	12 OZ.	7 OZ.	3 OZ.	1'2	2 OZ.	3 OZ.	1 LB.	16 PC
1942 FEB. 23	4 OZ.	8 OZ.	6 OZ.	2 OZ.	1'2	2 OZ.	3 OZ.	1 LB.	20 PC

MILK AND EGGS:
(PROPORTION ONLY, EXACT QUANTITIES VARYING)
ASSUMED ADULT ENTITLEMENT ➤ 3 PINTS OF MILK A WEEK   3 EGGS A MON

SPECIAL SUPPLIES: MILK —

EXPECTANT MOTHERS:	INFANTS:	CHILDREN:	INVALIDS: UP TO
7 PINTS	14 PINTS	3½ TO 7 PINTS	14 PINTS

12 EGGS A MC FOR CHILDR AND EXPECT MOTHERS

OTHER EXTRAS FOR CHILDREN: ORANGES | FRUIT JUICE CHILDREN UP TO TWO YEARS | COD LIVER OI CHILDREN UP TO SIX YEARS

HOW RATIONING DEVELOPED IN THREE YEARS OF WAR

Did you know?
Many children were sent
to the countryside.
This was to keep them safe
from the bombing raids
on the towns.

Index